PIGSKIN PARABLES

DEVOTIONS FROM THE GAME OF FOOTBALL
CANDEE FICK

DEDICATION

This devotional is dedicated to my son Luke. I still remember the day you got your first football ... and then shoved stuffed animals inside your shirt as pads so you could be a "real" football player.

May your faith surpass your love of the game.

CONTENTS

INTRODUCTION

A round our house, football reigns.

You see, my husband is a high school football coach. After teaching all day and running the team practice, he comes home to watch scouting films and scribble X's and O's on the nearest available pieces of paper. He relaxes on weekends by, what else, watching college and professional football games. Add free online fantasy leagues, a junior playing on his high school team, a 5th grader playing flag football at recess, and tackling practice in the middle of our living room . . .

So, what's a girl to do when surrounded by so much football? Watch and learn.

Learning about the game might help with dinner conversations and earn relationship points, but I'm talking about life in general. There are lessons to be learned and we'll be looking at several of them. The following is a collection of devotional readings inspired by previous posts on my blog at CandeeFick.com.

If you like these lessons about faith and life illustrated through the game of football, you might also like Book Two in the series. *Pigskin Parables: Exploring Faith and Football* is an eleven-week devotional with weekly topics, each with five days of targeted readings and practical application drills.

One last thing before we kick off. If you want to get email updates about new releases, appearances, and sales, you can also sign up for my newsletter at CandeeFick.com. I send out something about once a month and often there's free stuff included for my readers!

Focus on the Fundamentals

"'Teacher, which is the greatest commandment in the Law?' Jesus replied: 'Love the Lord your God with all your heart and with all your soul and with all your mind. This is the first and greatest commandment. And the second is like it: Love your neighbor as yourself.'" ~ Matthew 22:36-37

What season is this? Did you just you say fall? Well, technically it's still summer, but I'm thinking football season.

With a coaching husband and two boys, our household seems to revolve around the sport. After watching the game from the sidelines for years, I started seeing life lessons illustrated on the field. And wrote my first book (re-released as *Pigskin Parables: Exploring Faith and Football*) based on what I'd been learning. So, when football season arrives each year, my brain starts seeing the similarities again.

Take, for instance, this common coaching philosophy: Focus on the fundamentals.

Focus: Give deliberate attention to it. Zero in. Block out the distractions. Aim for. Keep in sight.

Fundamentals: The basic components and building blocks. The essential elements. Those things of major significance. The most important and foundational pieces.

In football, the fundamentals include throwing, catching, blocking, and tackling. Without the basic ability to execute the game plan, all the scouting and strategy falls apart.

In life, the fundamentals are harder to define, yet still as crucial. As I started thinking, three things jumped to the top of my list. Faith. Family. Stewardship (making the most of what I've been given including money, time, and talents). And wrapped around them is love. Love God and love others.

Simple? Maybe. But if I can do these few things well, the rest of my life should fall into place somewhere. Not that mastering the fundamentals is easy. That's why every coach spends time at every practice running the players through drills designed to keep the fundamental skills sharp. (Hence the word focus. It doesn't happen accidentally.)

But, in doing this, don't forget what my youngest son's flag football coach said. "We'll teach the boys the fundamentals of the game, but we also want them to have a good time." After all, check out the first three letters: F-U-N.

Focus on the fundamentals in life. And take time to relax and enjoy the journey.

> **What about you?**
> **What fundamentals are you focusing on? What do you do for fun?**

MAKE A CHOICE

"But if serving
the LORD seems
undesirable to you,
then choose for
yourselves this day
whom you will serve
... But as for me and
my household, we will
serve the LORD." ~
Joshua 24:15

After years coaching high school football, my husband spent a year volunteering at the college level. And the higher intensity game continued to teach me about life.

During the off-season, the coaching staff was busy recruiting.

They traveled the country and visited hundreds of schools to meet potential players. Back home, they evaluated film after film sent in by high school athletes eager to play at the next level. After ranking the possibilities, they hit the road again with specific targets in mind. They talked to kids about the football program. The university. The city. They invited players to attend summer camps and extended scholarship offers.

And then they waited.

Wait for the recruits to make a choice. To verbally commit. To officially sign their name on a letter of intent in February. To pack their bags and join the team for next year's spring and summer workouts.

Just because the coaches have offered a place on the team, doesn't mean that student will choose to come. So, they follow up the offer with visits, letters, and phone calls.

What does this have to do with life?

We've each been offered a place on the best team in the universe. To join a program whose philosophy is love. To execute plays like forgiveness, compassion, healing, truth. To combat the opponent's strategies of bitterness, hatred, pain, and deception. To live and work under an authority structure rooted in justice and mercy.

But we have to make a choice. Choosing one team automatically rejects another. So chose wisely.

What about you?
Have you made the choice? Are you recruiting your friends to join your team? Have you found that the other team is still trying to recruit you?

DOING THE MUNDANE

"... If anyone wants
to be first, he must be
the very last, and the
servant of all." ~Mark
9:35

I was watching a college football game last night on
television and I noticed something. Coaches wearing
headsets and carrying clipboards mingled with the team
on the sidelines. They sent in the play calls and talked to
their players after each series. And appeared on camera.

But behind them? Brief glimpses of others taping
ankles, icing injuries, and filling water bottles.

And further behind the scenes? Staff members washing
the uniforms, setting up the locker room, making travel
and lodging arrangements, ordering food, videotaping
games, and tagging game films on their computer system.

Every coaching staff has members willing to do the dirty work. To step up and do the stuff that has to be done, freeing other coaches to study film, strategize a new game plan, and lead the team meetings.

So, what's that gotta do with life? My husband and I are like the coaching staff of our family. (He's the head coach and I'm the assistant.) Together, we teach our kids the game plan for life and guide them toward the goal. And in the process of sharing this load, somebody has to handle the everyday stuff like laundry, meals, transportation, and checking homework.

And seen in that light, doing the mundane becomes a lot more important.

> **What about you?**
> **Are you part of a coaching staff? Do you lead some kind of team? Do you have a game plan? How important is the mundane?**

COACHES

"But the Counselor, the Holy Spirit, whom the Father will send in my name, will teach you all things and will remind you of everything I have said to you." ~ John 14:26

"Mentoring is a brain to pick, an ear to listen, and a push in the right direction." ~ John Crosby

Not only is my husband a coach, but I used to coach track and cross-country. (Not quite football but enough to show that I know of what I speak.)

The coach is the team leader and teacher. Responsible for the safety and conduct of the team. Commissioned with the task of teaching skill and building endurance in addition to developing a game plan and implementing changes from the sideline. Corrector. Encourager. Friend. One who shoulders the blame and passes along the credit while preparing the team for the next level of competition. The good ones have learned the game from others and lead by example.

The athletes who find quality coaches and listen to their instruction have an advantage over their peers. Those who don't? Well, a coach can only point you in the right direction. You have to listen and do the work yourself.

What about life? Successful travelers have coaches (also known as mentors, agents, and friends). Someone with more knowledge and experience who shares their wisdom and offers encouragement for the journey. Who can point out the potholes and steer in the right direction.

What about you?
Do you have a coach? Are you listening? Have you thanked them?

Training

"Therefore I do not run like a man running aimlessly; I do not fight like a man beating the air. No, I beat my body and make it my slave so that after I have preached to others, I myself will not be disqualified for the prize." ~ 1 Corinthians 9:26-27

"Those who work the hardest, who subject themselves to the strictest discipline, who give up certain pleasurable things in order to achieve a goal, are the happiest." ~ Brutus Hamilton, Olympic decathlete and coach

During the off-season, football programs continue strength and conditioning programs in addition to spring and/or summer camps.

Why? To prepare their bodies for the months ahead. But such training takes hard work and discipline.

I took a closer look at the word discipline. The definition of discipline is training that is expected to produce a specific character or pattern of behavior.

Training for a desired result.

For example, what if a player desires to run faster or lift a heavier weight? With the help of his coaches, they develop a plan of action and the player commits to pursing that goal through a lot of hard work. And every day he finds himself a little bit closer.

Would that make him happy? It should. Because he has a goal ... and a plan ... and is making progress. He is in training.

I might not be in physical training (although perhaps I should be!), but what patterns of behavior might I pursue? Spending more time in the Word. Loving my husband through his love language of words. Healthier eating habits. Spending one-on-one time with each of my children. Writing on a consistent basis with weekly word count goals.

However, having a goal is not enough.

I must have a plan and I must work at it regularly if I want to see any progress.

That's what training is all about.

What about you?
Are you in training? Do you think those in
training are the happiest? Why or why not?

THE WEIGHT ROOM

"We also rejoice in our sufferings, because we know that suffering produces perseverance; perseverance, character; and character, hope." ~ Romans 5:3-4

Today, we're going to look at the weight room. That place filled with clanging metal, loud supposedly-inspiring music, and sweating bodies. Where athletes grunt, groan, and strain to lift bars loaded with weights, and then do it again. And again.

Why would any sane person put themselves through such torture? To grow stronger. To build muscle. To run faster. To push harder. To face opposing linemen without flinching. To withstand injury.

How? Because repeatedly pushing against resistance builds strength. The athlete is then able to lift that same loaded bar with less effort than before. Or, they can increase the weight and take on a bigger challenge.

It's the same in life. Every time I successfully face resistance, I grow stronger in character. And faith. And patience. That increased strength comes in handy the next time I face opposition or trials.

Hmm. Rejoice in the weight room because it makes me stronger. That sounds familiar.

What about you?
What resistance are you facing? Are you growing stronger from the opposition or letting it keep you out of the weight room of life?

PAYING THE PRICE

"Let us fix our eyes on
Jesus, the author and
perfecter of our faith,
who for the joy set
before him endured
the cross, scorning its
shame, and sat down
at the right hand of
the throne of God." ~
Hebrews 12:2

I magine a football player attending every team meeting and participating in every practice or workout. Running wind-sprints. Hitting hard and making tackles. Lifting weights. And risking injury. Day in and day out, making the sacrifice for the team.

Sounds like a player doing what they're supposed to do. Someone who is carrying through on their commitment to the team.

But what if I said they made this level of sacrifice without a financial benefit or scholarship award? Such is the life of the college walk-on. (In fact, one young man in our area, despite great financial need, had to turn down a different scholarship in order to continue participating in football and not violate any rules.)

Why would these young men do this? For the love of the game and the opportunity to be part of something bigger than themselves. For the hope that someday, if they pay the price long enough, they may get the call elevating them from mere walk-on to scholarship player.

And that's worth the sacrifice.

(By the way, the young man who turned down another scholarship started this season as a junior walk-on. Due to other injuries on the team, he is now a scholarship player for the remainder of the year.)

What about me? Well, there are things I do faithfully every day without immediate reward. Granted, not all rewards are financial and not all are seen in this lifetime. But sacrifice happens when the joy of what is coming is greater than the pain of what is required. So, I'll continue to pay the price with my family, at home, on the job, and in my writing.

And hopefully I'll someday get "the call" from an agent or editor offering representation or a book contract.

> **What about you?**
> **What sacrifices have you made? What result are you hoping for? Is the coming joy greater than the pain?**

Strategize for Success

> "Do your best to present yourself to God as one approved, a workman who does not need to be ashamed and who correctly handles the word of truth ... Be prepared in season and out of season ..." ~ 2 Timothy 2:15; 4:2

One of the things my husband loves about coaching football is the strategic planning. Studying the opponent's game film looking for tendencies and weaknesses.

And designing corresponding play calls to capitalize on that information.

Despite only having a few kinds of plays (run, pass, kick), a team's playbook is filled with endless possibilities and variations. Some are used frequently throughout the game, while others are held for specific situations.

And all must be defended against.

Much of the practice time during the week is devoted to preparing the appropriate response, teaching it in team meetings, and rehearsing it against the scout team. When they do such-and-such, we will do such-and-such.

Over and over until the time comes to take the field and put the strategy into action.

It's the same in life. But instead of rushes and passes, we face deception and temptation.

How will we respond in the heat of battle? With the rehearsed response. And the simpler the better so we can remember it.

I have a basic defensive strategy. Respond in love. Speak the truth. Say "no" to temptation. Honor God in all I say and do.

My offensive strategy is simple too. Love God. Love others.

So, when the seven-year-old comes tattling because his thirteen-year-old brother just tackled him? When I'm leaving the gym after a good workout and drive past a McDonald's with the smell of French fries wafting on the breeze? When I've pushed hard all day to meet work deadlines and my husband asks me to do one more thing?

The secret to strategy is knowing what you may face and having a prepared response.

What about you?
What tendencies and weaknesses do you have in life? How are you defending against the attacks?

Teamwork

"Now the body is not
made up of one part
but of many ... If one
part suffers, every part
suffers with it; if one
part is honored, every
part rejoices with it." ~
1 Corinthians 12:14,
26

Teamwork divides the task and multiplies the
success. ~ Author unknown

I picked a particular image for the cover of my
book, *Pigskin Parables: Exploring Faith and Football,*

because it showed a team in action. Teammates huddled together and communicating the play call. Leaving to do their individual parts, and then returning to encourage or congratulate each other before doing it all over again.

In the game of football, each team has eleven players on the field. Count them. Not one or two, but eleven. Each with individual responsibilities on every play. One to snap the ball to the quarterback. Four additional linemen to protect the quarterback from various angles of attack and to open holes for the running backs. The receivers run assigned routes to either get in position to catch the ball or to draw the defensive players away from an area of the field. Running backs sometimes run with the ball and sometimes block for their teammates. The quarterback surveys the defense, adjusts the play call, and then throws or hands off the ball.

Eleven players, each with a small part of the overall task. None of them could do it alone, and each individual effort contributes to the success (or failure) of the team. (Not to mention the fact that other teammates cheer from the sidelines and stand ready to take their place on the field if someone is injured.)

Football is a team sport. So is life.

I can't do this by myself and I'd be crazy to try. I need my teammates as much as the quarterback needs his. Can you imagine if he tried to run a play by himself without anyone blocking for him? Ouch.

So, who's on my team? My husband. My parents. My friends. My daughter's doctor and speech therapist. Her teachers and paraprofessionals. My boys' teachers, coaches, Sunday School teachers, and youth group leaders. My critique partners and local writing group.

Not too long ago, I spent several days out of town at a writer's conference. While I was away from home, my mother stepped in to handle the daily details of three kids' school schedules and activities. Friends prayed for me. My critique partners helped me polish my first chapters and proposal. My roommate became a new friend to cheer me on before every appointment. I found members of my local writer's group there to listen during the rough spots. And my husband both subsidized and encouraged the pursuit of my dream.

Could I have done it without all their help? Not a chance.

What about you?
Who's on your team? Have you thanked them for their help? What are you doing to help them?

PICKING YOUR FANTASY TEAM

"If the whole body were an eye, where would the sense of hearing be? If the whole body were an ear, where would the sense of smell be?" ~ 1 Corinthians 12:17

My husband and oldest son are part of several (free) online fantasy football contests. Every week they check up on their chosen players, bench the injured ones, and occasionally trade a few out for someone with better on-field statistics. Then, every weekend they follow the sports news to see how their teams did.

How did they pick the players on their team? By carefully analyzing past performance and health histories.

Are they coming off an injury or are they strong? Are they getting most of the carries on their team or are they sharing the load with a group of running backs? How strong is their schedule this season? Will they be playing outside in Chicago or inside a dome in Minnesota?

After juggling the variables and adjusting for the fictional salary cap, they lock in their selections for the week. And hope that collectively the team comes through with a good game.

What about life? I'm part of several teams. My family at home. The company I work for. Writing critique groups. Each member of the team has strengths and weaknesses that affect their particular responsibilities. Hopefully, we balance each other out.

For example, I'm the organized one in our marriage, so I keep track of the family calendar, finances, and taxes while my husband's frugality keeps me accountable in the spending department. I'm horrible (but getting better) at punctuation and grammar rules, so I rely on a couple of my critique partners to catch my blunders. I read fast with good comprehension, so my boss sends me the largest cases because I can get them done quickly while others can glean full reports from minimal information.

So, here are a few questions to consider as you pick your real-life fantasy teams:

Who do you want on your team? Why? Do you seek after people because of their contributions? Their consistency? Their ability to push through the hard times by your side? Their willingness to go the extra mile? Or do you end up on teams with people who are takers, whiners, and easily injured?

What about you?
Who's on your team? And, perhaps most importantly, if given the choice, would your teammates pick you?

PROTECTING
FROM INJURY

"He heals the brokenhearted and binds up their wounds." ~ Psalm 147:3

L ife, like football, hits hard and so you'd better be protected.

In my book, *Pigskin Parables: Exploring Faith and Football*, I spend a chapter comparing football pads and the spiritual armor listed in Ephesians 6. I won't rehash the topic other than to say "PUT IT ON." Salvation, righteousness, truth, peace, and faith will cushion the inevitable blows in life.

But just because a player is wearing all their pads doesn't mean that injuries can't or won't happen.

Take for instance my thirteen-year-old son. While playing quarterback in a middle school game, he came down on one foot in time for a linebacker to plow into his lower leg. Rolling his ankle and resulting in a severe sprain.

What was the solution? We started off with the tried-and-true "R-I-C-E" method. Rest. Ice. Compression. Elevation. And after a weekend of treatment, he could walk semi-normally and jog a little.

Before he returned to practice, he strapped on a pair of ankle braces. For support while he continued to heal. And protection from future ankle-rolling incidents (of which there were several more opportunities).

In life, no matter how well protected we are, we still get hit. Blindsided. Knocked off our feet. Buried at the bottom of the pile. And beyond the bumps and bruises, we might even get injured in the process.

But we can rehab the injuries in similar ways. Prayer to reduce the inflammation and pain. Rest in the Father's loving arms. Lifting the injury up to let God do the healing. And wrapping the pain in a cocoon of faith that shores up our weaknesses and protects us during the healing process.

What about you?
Have you been injured by life's hits? What did your healing process look like?

BELIEVING YOUR PRESS

"The crucible for silver and the furnace for gold, but man is tested by the praise he receives." ~ Proverbs 27:21

One thing I've noticed while my husband was a part of football at the college level was that there is at least one newspaper article covering some aspect of the team every day. Every day. Not to mention the numerous radio and television reporters and commentators with their pre-game, game, and post-game coverage. Add in the mid-week coach's show and daily sports talk radio.

That's a lot of press. And a lot of chances, as a player, to see or hear your name mentioned.

Leading to today's dilemma. Is everything the press says accurate? No. They've been known to make the occasional mistake or misquote. Is everything they say flattering? Usually not! But suppose for a moment that it was. Would an all-positive press report be truly accurate?

The bottom line is that we all hear good and bad things about ourselves. The tricky part is learning what press to believe. All good and I risk an inflated ego. All bad and I wallow in self-pity.

The real truth lies somewhere in between. I do some stuff well and drop the ball when it comes to other things. Some days I'm a patient mother. And other days? Not so much. By listening to the good and bad — the praise and the criticism — I can identify areas for improvement and receive encouragement for the journey ahead. After all, we all need a few tidbits of praise to keep us going on the tough days.

What about you?
What has the press been saying lately about you?
Which variety do you tend to believe? How much
credibility do you give the critics?

PENALTIES

"... And you may be
sure that your sin
will find you out." ~
Numbers 32:23

I'm a busy mom of three children, ages seven to fourteen. By default, that also makes me the referee.

Somehow, I'm supposed to be aware of where everyone is at all times, what they are doing, and whom they are doing it to. I should be on hand to immediately step in and punish the misbehaving offender with the appropriate (predetermined) consequence without allowing my personal emotions to influence the outcome.

Yeah, right.

Like I have eyes in the back of my head or something. Like I'm never sleep-deprived, hormonal, or simply frustrated with the frequency of the offenses. Like I don't have other things (work, fixing supper or driving the car) or other people (my husband, the person on the phone, another child) to take care of. Like I always have the appropriate consequence ready to hand down.

So, I miss stuff. The guilty go unpunished and the innocent cry "unfair!" I'm sorry. It happens. And I'll try better next time.

The same can be said of the game of football. Twenty-two players on the field. Four referees. You do the math. Somebody is going to miss seeing something sometime. And somebody is going to think they saw something that didn't really happen. At least they've got the advantage of instant replay in certain situations.

But don't tell me that a sideline ref never gets ticked at being screamed at and maybe, just perhaps, is quicker to throw a flag on that team in retaliation. They're human too (even if the guy behind me at the last game I attended said they needed glasses).

The point? Life isn't fair. Not all the bad guys are caught or punished. And sometimes the innocent get caught in the cross-fire with unintentional consequences.

The real lesson comes in how I respond in the face of a flag (or no flag).

Do I acknowledge I made the mistake and accept the consequences? Do I continue my behavior since I didn't get caught last time? Do I complain when someone else gets away with an offense? Or do I rejoice when others get caught? And do I find reassurance in the fact there is an ultimate Judge upstairs watching every player?

What about you?
Are you the referee, the penalized, or both? How do you handle it when the bad guys get away with one? How do you respond when your mistake is overlooked?

PERSEVERANCE

"I have fought the
good fight, I have
finished the race, I
have kept the faith." ~
2 Timothy 4:7

Today I'd like to honor those who overcome the obstacles. Who keep getting up when knocked down. Who persevere despite the problems.

Football players have to be tough both mentally and physically. They are constantly shoved around or tackled to the ground. Forward progress is stopped by a strong defense. Or a mistake. Or a penalty. They continue to play no matter if they are outsized or outscored. Even the weather can conspire against them with wind, driving rain, or freezing drizzle.

A few years ago, my husband's team played in such a game. Our opponent was bigger, stronger, and faster than us at every position. They stifled our offense and ran away with the game, scoring at will until the "mercy rule" took effect with a running clock. Did I mention it was raining sheets of water - sideways - for the entire game?

Yet, I was so proud of our team and coaches. They never gave up. They left everything they had out there on the field. They slogged off the turf with heads held high, despite the tears in their eyes. And, paid the price during the off season to prepare for the next year's rematch.

What about life? Obstacles and failure are as much a part of life as tackles and fumbles exist in football. The key is what you do next. Will you buckle under the pressure or continue to pursue your dream? If you need more inspiration, search You-Tube for a video from BlueFish TV about Famous Failures. (Warning - bring a tissue)

What about you?
When you face opposition, do you give in? Or do you persevere?

TIME OUT

"Then, because so many people were coming and going that they did not even have a chance to eat, he said to them, 'Come with me by yourselves to a quiet place and get some rest.'" ~ Mark 6:31

T he game of football is full of pushing and shoving along the line of scrimmage, bursts of action, crushing hits, and running back to the huddle to do it again.

And again.

CANDEE FICK

A physical battle is waged over ball possession, field position, and points. Emotions run high, and sweat pours from athletes giving everything they have play after play after play.

Until the whistle blows.

"Time out called by the home team."

The teams head for a sideline huddle. Managers rush over with water bottles. Coaches make crucial decisions and issue new instructions. Players catch their breath.

When the brief but necessary time is up, they head back into battle.

What about us? Do you ever feel like you're in a shoving match or being tackled to the ground by life's circumstances? Like you're in a battle of brief skirmishes or sustained drives? Like your energy is being drained even as you devote yourself to the task at hand?

Call a time out.

Catch your breath and regain your perspective on priorities. Rehydrate yourself with activities that fill you up. Weigh your options and make well-informed decisions. Get advice, correction, or encouragement from your coaches or teammates. Make adjustments to my strategy.

Then get back in the game.

Oh, and should I mention that football also has scheduled times of rest (aka half-time)? You don't see players strutting around like rest is for weaklings or begging to stay out on the field because they have too much to do.

If even muscular trained athletes need a break, how much more does this frazzled mom need to call a time out?

So, when life comes at you fast, remember to call a time out. Your sanity will thank you.

What about you?
When was the last time you needed to call a time-out? How long did it last? Did it help? What is your favorite form of rehydration? And, what's your biggest excuse for not resting?

VICTORY IS
SWEETER

> "I tell you that in the
> same way there will
> be more rejoicing in
> heaven over one sinner
> who repents than over
> ninety-nine righteous
> persons who do not
> need to repent." ~
> Luke 15:7

Victory is sweeter ... when the battle has been fierce and the journey has been long.

Last fall, I attended a college football game with my (then) twelve-year-old son, my dad, and my brother while my husband watched from the press box. The Colorado State University Rams faced off against the Idaho Vandals in a stadium filled with retro-uniform orange. Beautiful weather. A spirited band with a chorus line of suicide trombones. Cannon fire after each home team score along with Cam, the ram, being trotted across the end zone. And hopes were high since CSU had a 12-game losing streak going in.

The game was intense as each team exchanged points, the lead, and the momentum. And then in the 4th quarter, CSU scored yet another touchdown. The extra point to tie the game? Missed. Trailing into the final minutes, the crowd helped the defense with a critical stop and the offense took the field for the two-minute drill. Leading to a field goal attempt with 3 seconds left on the clock.

A field goal that split the uprights, securing the victory and snapping the streak. The first win of the year and the first win in over a year.

Watching the team celebrate on the field, I was reminded that the harder the battle, the sweeter the victory. And the longer the journey, the more satisfying the destination.

Working extra hours for three years to pay off a debt? Skipping favorite television shows and writing into the night to finish the rough draft of a novel? Spending hours with physical and speech therapists to help your child walk, run, and talk? Changing your lifestyle and habits to recover from a chronic illness? Sticking with my husband through the better and worse to build a strong marriage? Making the daily choices to live out my faith in a culture that denies God's existence or relevance?

Easy? Never. But the victory is sweeter for the struggle.

What about you?
What motivates you during the long struggles of life? Do you have any recent victories to share?

THE REWARD

"I the LORD search the heart and examine the mind, to reward a man according to his conduct, according to what his deeds deserve." ~ Jeremiah 17:10

As the weeks countdown to the end of the college football season, sportscasters actively debate the intricacies and merits of the various post-season college bowl games and awards.

Who is in the running for the Heisman trophy? Who will be playing for the National Championship according to the BCS (Bowl Championship Series) computer and who should be? Who faced the toughest opponents, who won with the greatest point margins, and whose statistics are more impressive?

It's all about comparisons ... and extremely complex mathematical calculations. And those who come out on top get trophies, rings, national attention, and the chance to keep playing into the new year (and at the next level).

But what about those teams or players who end up just a bit further down the list? Are they any less worthy of recognition for their efforts?

When it comes to life, I sometimes feel like I'm being judged by equally complex calculations. How clean is my house? How polite are my kids? How physically fit am I and how out-of-date is my wardrobe? Do I volunteer at my child's school or our church? How many verses can I quote? How have my trials compared with those others have faced? Have I overcome the setbacks as easily as someone else did?

When I take a closer look, I realize I'm the one doing the judging. And I don't even know the true criteria!

Instead, when it comes to post-earthly-life rewards, I can rest in the knowledge that the One who sees all and knows everything is one passing out the true rewards.

What about you?

Do you struggle with comparisons? Do you find hope knowing that God is the ultimate Judge? What would be the best reward you can dream of?

Dear Reader,

Thank you for spending a few hours of your time with me. I hope you enjoyed exploring a few life lessons from the game of football.

There is no greater pleasure as an author than knowing that I've encouraged my readers! If you enjoyed this book, please take a few minutes to let the rest of the world know by leaving a review at your favorite retailer or on sites like Goodreads or BookBub. It doesn't have to be long. Just a few words pointing other readers this direction would be much appreciated. Better yet, maybe even tell others about your favorite life lesson from football.

In fact, you might also like Book Two in the series, *Pigskin Parables: Exploring Faith and Football*. It's an eleven-week long devotional journey that looks deeper into subjects including coaching, preparation, strategy, teamwork, protection, rules and consequences, criticism, perseverance, time outs and rewards. Each week's topic includes five daily readings and practical application drills.

In addition to writing non-fiction and devotionals, I also write Christian romance. Since you've already shown an interest in football, you might enjoy my debut novel involving a behind-the-scenes look at a college football program. *Catch of a Lifetime*, an inspirational romance, tells the story of a rookie coach and bitter tutor who must overcome stereotypes and work together to salvage the season when his star receiver teeters on the brink of ineligibility. Their growing relationship must remain hidden behind a wall of professionalism, but when a scandal erupts, the aftermath could cost both of their careers.

If you'd like to receive updates about upcoming books or sales, you can sign up for email list on my website at CandeeFick.com. (There might be a few surprises headed your way including a free novella and other exclusive bonus content.)

As I continue to write stories of faith, hope, and love, my prayer is that you will experience the amazing love of God and find encouragement for the journey called life.

Until we (hopefully) meet again in the pages of a book, happy reading everyone!

Candee

MORE NON-FICTION

A complete and up-to-date list of all my books
(including my novels) can be found on my website at
CandeeFick.com

DEVOTIONALS

Pigskin Parables: Devotions from the Game of Football

Pigskin Parables: Exploring Faith and Football

Devotions from the Garden

Be Like a Tree

Creation Declares

With All of Creation – compilation boxset

OTHER NON-FICTION

Making Lemonade: Parents Transforming Special Needs

The Author Toolbox

PREVIEW: PIGSKIN PARABLES

Kick off a season of spiritual growth with this eleven-week devotional journey exploring what faith and football have in common.

As the wife of a high school football coach, author Candee Fick has climbed metal bleachers in all kinds of weather to see firsthand the battle for field position and points. In addition to discovering the benefits of a comfortable stadium chair, she has seen many lessons about life illustrated on the playing field including coaching, preparation, strategy, teamwork, protection, criticism, rules and consequences, perseverance, time outs, and rewards.

This updated and reformatted version of an earlier book combines aspects of the game of football, personal anecdotes, practical examples, and Scripture to illustrate biblical truths about life.

Each week includes an introduction, five daily readings, application drills, and a topic review.

About Candee

C andee Fick is a multipublished, award-winning author. She is also the wife of a high school football coach and the mother of three children, including a daughter with a rare genetic syndrome. When not busy writing, editing, or coaching other authors, she can be found exploring the great Colorado outdoors, indulging in dark chocolate, and savoring happily-ever-after endings through a good book.

Visit her website at CandeeFick.com where you can find out about her latest releases and sign up for her email list.

www.ingramcontent.com/pod-product-compliance
Lightning Source LLC
Chambersburg PA
CBHW032113040426
42337CB00040B/523